Unbelievable Pictures and Facts About Norway

By: Olivia Greenwood

Introduction

Norway is a country that is filled with museums, wooden houses and lots of mountains. It is a wonderful place to go if you enjoy fishing or skiing. We will be learning all about the wonderful country of Norway.

On average what is the life expectancy in Norway?

In Noway people usually live long and healthy lives. On average the people in Norway live up until 85 years of age.

Will you find any rivers in Norway?

Yes, you will certainly find many rivers that run through the country of Norway.

Which languages do people in Norway speak?

In Norway, people speak a variety of different languages. They speak Norwegian and a language called Sami.

Will you find any forests in Norway?

Yes, you will certainly find some beautiful and unique forests in Norway.

Which sport do people enjoy the most in Norway?

The sport which people love the most in Norway is soccer. Everyone in the country loves soccer and some people are really good at it too.

What items do they export to other countries?

The items which are exported the most from Norway to other countries are fish fillets and raw aluminum.

What type of education do they offer in Norway?

The education which is offered in Norway is really excellent. Norway is known for having a top education system. People from all over the world come to study in Norway.

Which religion is followed the most in the country?

In the country of Norway, the religion which is followed the most is Christianity.

What do the people in the country like to eat?

In Noway they like to eat all sorts of meat such as duck and deer. They also really enjoy seafood. The oceans are in close proximity so it is very easy to get fresh seafood to eat.

Does the country have a national flower of its own?

The country does have its own national flower. The name of this flower is the purple heather. These flowers are really beautiful and can be seen all over the country.

What type of money do they use in the country?

If you wish to buy things in Norway you will need to make use of the Norwegian Kroner. This is the official financial currency of the country.

What is the population size in Norway?

Norway is home to nearly 5,446,780 people. There are many people living in Norway.

Which city is the capital one?

Oslo is the name of the capital city. It is home to millions of people. It is also one of the most expensive cities in the entire world.

Is Norway a country that has lots of money?

Norway is a country that has lots of money. It does very well in the economy. It also is one of the largest oil exporters in the entire world.

Are there many museums in Norway?

Do you like going to museums? Museums are always a fun way to learn about important places and things. In Norway, you will find many museums.

What is the weather like in Norway?

Each season in Norway is completely different. During the wintertime it will get very cold. During the summer months, it has a tendency to warm and be much more pleasant.

Is Norway a big country or a small one?

In terms of size, Norway is actually a very big country. It is ranked as one of the bigger countries in the world.

Where in the world is Norway located?

Do you know where to find Northern Europe on the map? If you are able to locate Northern Europe you will be able to find the country of Norway.

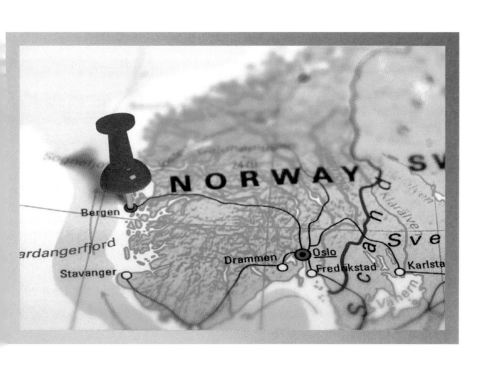

What type of geography is there in Norway?

Norway is surrounded by islands, lakes, rivers, mountains and stunning valleys. The country has truly beautiful landscapes and scenery.

Is it safe to travel in Norway?

Norway is a very safe country, especially compared to many other places. You will be safe and secure traveling in Norway.

Made in the USA
San Bernardino, CA
04 August 2020